YAMATONADESHIKO SHICHIHENGE

♥ 6 ♥

Tomoko Hayakawa

TRANSLATED AND ADAPTED BY
David Ury

LETTERED BY
Dana Hayward

BALLANTINE BOOKS • NEW YORK

2005 Del Rey® Trade Paperback Edition

Copyright © 2006 Tomoko Hayakawa.

Published in the United States by Del Rey Books, an imprint of The Random House Publishing Group, a division of Random House Inc., New York.

DEL REY is a registered trademark and the Del Rey colophon is a trademark of Random House, Inc.

Originally published in Japan in 2002 by Kodansha Ltd., Tokyo as *Yamatonadeshiko Shichihenge*.

This publication: rights arranged through Kodansha Ltd.

Library of Congress Control Number: 2004095918

ISBN 0-345-48370-7

Printed in the United States of America

www.delreymanga.com

9 8 7 6 5 4 3

Translator and adapter—David Ury

Lettering—Dana Hayward

Cover design—David Stevenson

Contents

A Note from the Author   iv

Honorifics   v

The Wallflower, Volume 6   1

Bonus Manga   168

About the Creator   176

Translation Notes   177

Preview of Volume 7   182

A Note from the Author

...BABIES
(A FEW
OF THEM)

MY...

♥ I heard from a friend that the late night TV show "Ranku Oukoku" ("The Kingdom of Ranking") listed *Wallflower* Volume 5 in their ranking. (I was so sad that I didn't get to see it myself . . . crying) It's all thanks to you guys. Thank you so much. ♥ ♥ ♥ I'll continue to do my best!
                                                              —Tomoko Hayakawa

Honorifics

Throughout the Del Rey Manga books, you will find Japanese honorifics left intact in the translations. For those not familiar with how the Japanese use honorifics, and more important, how they differ from American honorifics, we present this brief overview.

Politeness has always been a critical facet of Japanese culture. Ever since the feudal era, when Japan was a highly stratified society, use of honorifics—which can be defined as polite speech that indicates relationship or status—has played an essential role in the Japanese language. When addressing someone in Japanese, an honorific usually takes the form of a suffix attached to one's name (example: "Asuna-san"), or as a title at the end of one's name or in place of the name itself (example: "Negi-sensei," or simply "Sensei!").

Honorifics can be expressions of respect or endearment. In the context of manga and anime, honorifics give insight into the nature of the relationship between characters. Many translations into English leave out these important honorifics, and therefore distort the "feel" of the original Japanese. Because Japanese honorifics contain nuances that English honorifics lack, it is our policy at Del Rey not to translate them. Here, instead, is a guide to some of the honorifics you may encounter in Del Rey Manga.

-san: This is the most common honorific, and is equivalent to Mr., Miss, Ms., Mrs., etc. It is the all-purpose honorific and can be used in any situation where politeness is required.

-sama: This is one level higher than "-san" and it is used to confer great respect.

-dono: This comes from the word "tono," which means "lord." It is an even higher level than "-sama," and confers utmost respect.

-kun: This suffix is used at the end of boys' names to express familiarity or endearment. It is also sometimes used by men among friends, or when addressing someone younger or of a lower station.

-chan: This is used to express endearment, mostly toward girls. It is also used for little boys, pets, and even among lovers. It gives a sense of childish cuteness.

Bozu: This is an informal way to refer to a boy, similar to the English term "kid" or "squirt."

Sempai/senpai: This title suggests that the addressee is one's "senior" in a group or organization. It is most often used in a school setting, where underclassmen refer to their upperclassmen as "sempai." It can also be used in the workplace, such as when a newer employee addresses an employee who has seniority in the company.

Kohai: This is the opposite of "sempai," and is used toward underclassmen in school or newcomers in the workplace. It connotes that the addressee is of lower station.

Sensei: Literally meaning "one who has come before," this title is used for teachers, doctors, or masters of any profession or art.

[blank]: Usually forgotten in these lists, but perhaps the most significant difference between Japanese and English. The lack of honorific means that the speaker has permission to address the person in a very intimate way. Usually, only family, spouses, or very close friends have this kind of permission. Known as *yobisute,* it can be gratifying when someone who has earned the intimacy starts to call one by one's name without an honorific. But when that intimacy hasn't been earned, it can be very insulting.

CONTENTS

Chapter 23
Oh, My Sweet Home! (Final Chapter)   3

Chapter 24
Forever Old Friends   49

Chapter 25
You Are More Beautiful Than a Rose   91

Chapter 26
Diving Panic   129

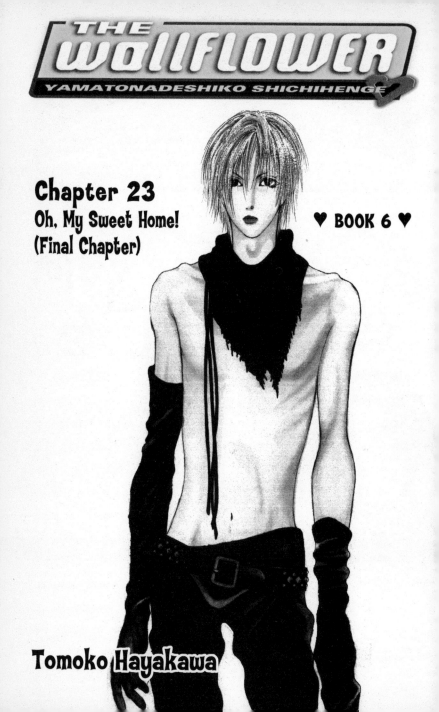

WALLFLOWER'S BEAUTIFUL CAST OF CHARACTERS (?)

SUNAKO IS A DARK LONER WHO LOVES HORROR MOVIES. WHEN HER AUNT, THE LANDLADY OF A BOARDING HOUSE, LEAVES TOWN WITH HER BOYFRIEND, SUNAKO IS FORCED TO LIVE WITH FOUR HANDSOME GUYS. SUNAKO'S AUNT MAKES A DEAL WITH THE BOYS, WHICH CAUSES NOTHING BUT HEADACHES FOR SUNAKO. "MAKE SUNAKO INTO A LADY, AND YOU CAN LIVE RENT-FREE."

BUT...HOW IS IT THAT THESE FOUR "CREATURES OF THE LIGHT" CAME TO LIVE TOGETHER IN THE SAME HOUSE? YOU'RE ABOUT TO FIND OUT IN THIS TALE OF DRAMA AND SUSPENSE.

SUNAKO NAKAHARA

TAKENAGA ODA—
CARING FEMINIST.

RANMARU MORII—
A TRUE LADIES' MAN.

KYOHEI TAKANO—
A STRONG FIGHTER,
"I'M THE KING."

YUKINOJO TOYAMA—
A GENTLE, CHEERFUL
AND VERY
EMOTIONAL GUY.

LET ME PUT IT THIS WAY. YOU WEREN'T JUST A LITTLE *"POCKET KNIFE."*

WHAT DO YOU MEAN, *"A WALKING BUTCHER KNIFE"*?

GRR

WHAT WAS I THINKING? HE'S JUST A CREATURE OF THE LIGHT.

HMMPH!

WHAT?

STIRRING

A BUTCHER KNIFE? ♥

BEHIND THE SCENES

WELL...I WAS PLANNING ON WRITING A "BEHIND THE SCENES," BUT I DON'T EVEN WANT TO THINK ABOUT IT...I'M SORRY. I WAS EMOTIONALLY UNSTABLE. AND...

THE SADS CONCERT WAS TWO DAYS BEFORE MY DEADLINE, SO I COULDN'T GO...
AHH...

MY MIND AND BODY WERE BOTH A MESS. IF ONLY I'D BEEN ABLE TO CATCH JUST A GLIMPSE OF KIYOHARU...SIGH...I CAUSED MY MOTHER AND LITTLE BROTHER A LOT OF TROUBLE. (ESPECIALLY MY BROTHER) MY LITTLE BROTHER IS SO SWEET. HE'S A REALLY GREAT GUY. (OR IS IT JUST SISTERLY LOVE?) I HOPE HE FINDS A CUTE WIFE SOON...I WANT A LITTLE SISTER. ♥

YOU SURE ARE LATE.

I'M HOME.

YEAH WELL, I PICKED SOMETHING UP ALONG THE WAY.

COME ON IN.

YOU...

...ARRIVED ON A STORMY DAY.

SAY HELLO.

SO SHE PICKED UP...

A PERSON?

THIS IS KYOHEI TAKANO-KUN. HE'LL BE YOUR NEW *ROOMMATE* AS OF TODAY.

RUMBLE RUMBLE

CRACK

TSSSSSSSS

FWIP

HEY.

WHOA! HE'S GOT A GREAT VOICE TOO.

HE'S GOT SCARY-LOOKING EYES, THOUGH.

HE'S SO HANDSOME. SO HANDSOME.

WOW, WOW!

GRR

ARE YOU SELLING ME TO THESE GUYS?

OR ARE YOU SELLING THEM, TOO?

THAT'S ENOUGH. NOW GO TAKE A BATH.

THERE'S A TOWEL AND A ROBE LAID OUT FOR YOU.

DO I LOOK LIKE A PIMP TO YOU?

WE'RE NOT BUYING YOU, AND WE SURE AS HELL AREN'T SELLING YOU!

DO I LOOK LIKE A CRIMINAL?

YEAH, YOU GOT THAT RIGHT, PRINCE.

RIGHT, YOUR HIGHNESS?

THAT GUY REALLY PISSES ME OFF!

OKAY.

CHATTER CHATTER

SLAM

Calm and cool.

HE PISSES ME OFF, TOO.

LOOKS LIKE THINGS ARE ABOUT TO GET INTERESTING.

GRR.

ふー
FUU

HOW CAN HE BE SO CALM?

パタン...
SLAM

HUH?

HEY, HEY, YOU'VE GOT A VISITOR ALREADY.

HE SAYS HE'S THE MANAGER FROM YOUR OLD JOB.

HE SAID YOU QUIT WITHOUT EVEN SAYING ANYTHING.

HE WAS WORRIED, SO HE CAME BY LOOKING FOR YOU.

HE WAS HANGING AROUND THE FRONT DOOR.

FWACK

CRUNCH

I NEVER WANNA SEE YOUR UGLY FACE AGAIN!

KYAA! KYAA! KYAA! KYAA!

TAP

SHIVER

DON'T YOU THINK THAT'S A BIT—

PLOINK

HE'S SO SCARY. SO SCARY!

H-HEY! WHAT THE HELL ARE YOU DOING?

WHAT?

IF YOU'VE GOT SOMETHING TO SAY, THEN SAY IT.

WHAT?

NOTHING.

HMM...

ｸ
ｸ
HEH.

HE SUDDENLY DISAPPEARED AND I DON'T KNOW WHAT TO DO.

I'M HIS *GIRL-FRIEND!*

YEAH RIGHT.

FWACK

AH!

COME ON! BRING HIM OUT HERE. ♥

ARE YOU A FRIEND OF KYOHEI TAKANO-KUN'S?

WHAT A CUTE GUY. ♥

HEY...

WHAT THE HELL?

HISS

HISS

NO, YOU'RE NOT! I AM!

I'M HIS REAL GIRL-FRIEND!

WHAT DO YOU MEAN YOU'RE HIS GIRL-FRIEND?

NO, I AM!

BUT HE'S JUST A NORMAL JUNIOR HIGH SCHOOL KID!

I HIRED A *PRIVATE EYE.*

THAT'S WHAT EVERYBODY DOES.

EH?

HEY...

HOW DID YOU KNOW THAT KYOHEI TAKANO-KUN WAS HERE?

AH, SHE LOOKS NORMAL ENOUGH.

WHAT?

WHERE WE COME FROM, KYOHEI-KUN IS EVEN MORE FAMOUS THAN KIMUTAKU.

WE LIVE IN A PRETTY SMALL TOWN.

WHOA, WHAT A CUTE GUY. ♥

I TRIED GOING TO HIS HOUSE, BUT THERE'S ALWAYS SOMEONE THERE WHO TURNS ME AWAY.

AND THERE'S ALWAYS A COP GUARDING HIM WHEN HE WALKS HOME FROM SCHOOL.

I NEVER GET A CHANCE TO TALK TO HIM.

WH-WHY IS ALL THAT NECESSARY?

HE'S ALWAYS QUITTING HIS JOBS, TOO... 'CAUSE OF SEXUAL HARASSMENT.

THAT'S WHY HIS MOM HAD A NERVOUS BREAK-DOWN.

I HEARD HE GETS KIDNAPPED ALL THE TIME.

THEY EVEN USE CHLOROFORM ON HIM.

I DON'T KNOW WHY EXACTLY, BUT...

RIP

WE MIGHT AS WELL READ THEM, RIGHT?

I'M SURE HE WON'T EVEN ACCEPT THEM, SO...

DESPICABLE.

LOOK HOW MANY LETTERS WERE IN THE MAIL-BOX.

SO THAT'S WHY HE ATTACKED THAT GUY WHO CAME OVER.

NOW IT ALL MAKES SENSE.

STOP, STOP! IT'S TOO SCARY!

OUCH. OUCH.

"TH- THIS IS HOW MUCH I LOVE YOU." ...?

ざぁ。
FWIP

KYAAAA!

↑ hair

OH, THIS IS A GOOD ONE.

ピ° RIP ピ° RIP
!! !!

HOW ABOUT THIS ONE?

Every time I see your warm smile... I'm filled with joy ♥

Knowing that you exist makes my life worth living.

I love you. I love you.
I love you. I love you.
I love you. I love you.

I've already planned our wedding. I can't wait ♥

I LOVE YOU

← Written in blood.

I've been waiting so long for you to come to me. Why won't you come to me?

WHY ARE YOU CRYING, MAN?

ズ—
SNIFF

IT'S ... IT'S JUST SO HORRIBLE.

HE ISN'T SAFE ANYWHERE.

ARE YOU ...

WHY DON'T YOU TRY AND SHOW A LITTLE MORE RESPECT...

...WHEN PEOPLE TRY TO HELP YOU.

YOU UNGRATEFUL LITTLE—

...LOOKING FOR A FIGHT?

WAHH!

NO.

CAN'T YOU JUST TRY BEING A LITTLE MORE APPRECIATIVE?

MY HERO. ♥

RING

GO HOME! GO HOME!

KYOHEI TAKANO-KUN DOESN'T LIVE HERE ANYMORE.

HE LEFT.

DON'T BOTHER LOOKING FOR HIM.

HELLO? NO, HE'S NOT HERE.

RING

GO AHEAD, BRING IT ON!

ATTENTION! EVERYBODY STANDING BY THE GATE!

bullhorn

OF COURSE, KYOHEI WON'T EVEN GIVE HIM THE TIME OF DAY.

HE REALLY IS A CUTIE.

THAT A BOY, YUKI-CHAN.

KYOHEI TAKANO IS NO LONGER HERE! PLEASE, RETURN TO YOUR HOMES IMMEDIATELY!

— 23 —

I SAW A SHADOW ON THE WINDOW THAT LOOKED JUST LIKE KYOHEI-KUN'S.

THEY'RE TOTALLY HIDING HIM, DON'T YOU THINK?

HEY...

WE'VE GOT TO FIND OUT FOR SURE!

YOU'RE AMAZING, YUKI-CHAN. ♥

THEY'RE ALL GONE.

NOW I CAN FINALLY RELAX AND GO ON MY DATE.

BYE! I'LL BE BACK LATER IN THE EVENING.

YEAH, LIKE ANYTHING WAS REALLY GONNA STOP YOU FROM YOUR DATE.

HEH.

HMM...

THERE'S GOT TO BE A WAY TO GET THEM OUT OF HERE.

IT DOESN'T EVEN FAZE HIM.

UHH, THIS SUCKS. GOD DAMN IT!

UGH...

I'M SICK OF ALL OF THIS.

HUH?

COME ON, PRINCE! THAT'S YOUR CUE.

THAT'S IT!

THEY JUST NEED SOMEONE TO CHASE AFTER.

IT DOESN'T EVEN HAVE TO BE ME.

GIGGLE

KYAA!

THAT'S THE SPIRIT!

WHEN YOU PUT IT THAT WAY, I GUESS I HAVE NO CHOICE.

TIME TO GET BUSY.

YOU'RE THE ONLY ONE WHO CAN SHUT THEM UP!

YOU'RE **SUPER SEXY**. ♥

...AND THAT HOT BODY...

YOUR PRETTY FACE...

...YOUR SILKY SMOOTH SKIN...

WITH YOUR BEAUTIFUL ORANGE-STREAKED HAIR AND...

— 28 —

サラサラ
FWIP
FWIP

ほ○ BLUSH...

キラキラキラ
SPARKLE
SPARKLE

ニニ GRIN

I'VE GOT PLENTY OF FREE TIME.

はぁー
AHH...

OKAY, I'VE GOT IT.

WHAT SHOULD WE DO? I'M NOT SEXY ENOUGH...

BUT THERE'RE STILL TONS OF THEM OUT THERE.

UH... UM...

ブクブク

GLUG
GLUG
GLUG

...TOLD THEM TO GO BACK HOME.

I ASKED FOR THEIR PHONE NUMBERS, AND...

はぁっ HAHH
はぁっ HAHH
はぁっ HAHH

← They ripped off his shirt.

YOU'RE AMAZING, PRINCE. ♥ WOW.

— 29 —

WHY DIDN'T YOU TELL US THAT THE CHIEF OF POLICE ASKED YOU TO TAKE CARE OF HIM?

I JUST DIDN'T KNOW WHERE TO START.

YOU KNEW WHAT WOULD HAPPEN, DIDN'T YOU?

THAT WAS PRETTY COOL.

YOU GOT DOWN ON YOUR KNEES AND BEGGED.

SHUT UP.

WALKING
BUTCHER
KNIFE

Chapter 24
Forever Old Friends

BEHIND THE SCENES

UNLIKE LAST TIME, I WAS TOTALLY HAPPY ♥ WHEN I WROTE THIS. I WAS IN THE MIDDLE OF CHANGING MY PERSONALITY AND MY LIFESTYLE. (I ENDED UP NOT CHANGING ANYTHING.) MY LITTLE DWARFS DID ALL THE INKING FOR ME WHILE I WAS ASLEEP. THESE TWO DWARFS ARE NAMED AYU WATANABE AND MACHIKO SAKURAI. ♥

HAVING TWO CUTE YOUNG GIRLS AROUND MAKES THE OFFICE FEEL MUCH MORE LIVELY. ♥ (THEY'RE BOTH BISHOUJO GIRLS.) THEIR FACES ARE REALLY SMALL. I HOPE NO ONE IS COMPARING THEIR LOOKS WITH MINE.

KYA! KYA!

HOW NICE TO BE SO YOUNG AND CUTE.

AN OLD LADY AND AN OLD MAN ENCHANTED BY YOUTH. (ME AND THE GENIUS HANA-CHAN.)

AFTER WORK, MACHIKO SAKURAI AND I WENT AROUND TO LOTS OF DIFFERENT TOY STORES. IT WAS FUN.

TIP TOE

?

KYAAA!

SPIN SPIN

A HA'PENNY PER FLOWER...
A HA'PENNY PER FLOWER.

MUMBLE MUMBLE

SPIN

WHY?

DI-DID SHE GET A JOB?... WORKING FROM HOME?

WHERE'S SHE FROM?

IT MUST BE FROM A VERY CLOSE FRIEND.

HOKKAIDO.

THUD

WOBBLE

"I WANT TO TALK TO YOU ABOUT SOMETHING. PLEASE COME VISIT. YUKI"

IS THAT WHAT THIS IS ABOUT?

ZZZZ

BONK BONK BONK

HEY, GIVE IT BACK!

— 52 —

HOKKAIDO. ♡

CRAB

THE NORTHERN FOX.

THE FIELDS OF LAVENDER.

THE CUTE GIRLS OF SAPPORO CITY.

SCALLOPS

SEA URCHIN

RING

IT'S AMAZING HOW OBSESSED SHE IS WITH THE PURSUIT OF BEAUTY.

WE'RE WORRIED ABOUT THE IDEA OF HER TRAVELING BY HERSELF, BUT...WHAT CAN WE DO?

SHE JUST WANTS TO GO ON THAT *SPA TOUR* SO BADLY.

BECAUSE SUNAKO-CHAN WORKED SO HARD AT HER *NEW JOB* THAT SHE COLLAPSED.

WHAT? WHY AM I CRYING?

AND, ACTION!

THE- THE LAND- LADY. ♥

NICE TIMING. ♥

WOW!

HOKKAIDO IS ALRIGHTO! ♥

HOW MANY GIRLS HAVE BEEN TRICKED BY THAT ACT?

SHE SAID SHE'D SEND CASH RIGHT AWAY! ♥

FOR ALL OF US.

HYUUUU

OKAY.

HOW SELFISH!

YOU ONLY BROUGHT YOUR OWN JACKET?

YOINK

ずぼ

bag

WHAT IS THIS? OUTER SPACE?

I MEAN IT'S PRACTI-CALLY THE BEGINNING OF SUMMER, RIGHT?

I-ISN'T IT SUPPOSED TO BE SPRING RIGHT NOW?

EXPLAIN THAT ONE.

WHY IS THERE STILL SNOW EVERYWHERE?

ガチ SHIVER
ガチ
ガチ SHIVER
ガチ
ガチ SHIVER
ガチ
ガチ SHIVER
ガチ

HEY...

SHUFFLE SHUFFLE
スタスタスタスタ

IF YOU DON'T LIKE IT, THEN GO HOME.

あ CLOP
ぼ
あ CLOP
ぼ

WE'RE HERE.

SUNAKO ?

ギ... CREEK

トン KNOCK
トン KNOCK

IT-IT LOOKS HAUNTED ...

YOU BROUGHT SOME FRIENDS?

IT'S BEEN SO LONG.

I MISSED YOU SO MUCH, SUNAKO!

MY MOM AND DAD WENT AWAY ON A TRIP.

PLEASE MAKE YOURSELF AT HOME.

THIS PLACE ISN'T MUCH, BUT...

COME ON IN.

MOVED ♥

IF YOU WERE AS CUTE AS HER, MAYBE WE'D BE A LITTLE NICER TO YOU.

SHE-SHE'S SO CUTE. ♥

WHOA.

DON'T BOTHER.

MY NAME IS YUKI, TOO. NICE TO MEET YOU.

WE HAVE THE SAME NAME.

LET'S SHAKE.

KYAAAA!

カチーン

KACHINK

ひやり

FREEZZZE

OH DEAR, HE'S FALLEN ASLEEP.

ACTUALLY, YUKI-CHAN'S NAME IS WRITTEN "SNOW WOMAN," BUT IT'S PRONOUNCED "YUKIME."

IT'S THE SNOW WOMAN. THE ABOMINABLE SNOW WOMAN!

SHE'S NOT EVEN SURPRISED!

YU-YUKI! YUKI!

I'M NOT THE ABOMINABLE SNOW WOMAN.

じょぼじょぼ

GLUB GLUB

—57—

THAT WAS MY GRANDMA.

WAHHH!
わああん

WE'RE GOING HOME!

DON'T CRY, YUKI-CHAN.

SUNAKO WAS THE ONLY ONE WHO UNDER-STOOD ME...

I COULD NEVER MAKE ANY FRIENDS.

THAT'S WHY... THAT'S WHY...

ぽろ ぽろ
DRIP DRIP

AWW... SUNAKO-CHAN IS SO SWEET.

SNIFF SNIFF

WHA-?
はっ

— 58 —

— 59 —

AHH...

HOKKAIDO. ♥

FLOP

FLIP
FLOP

WHA-
WHAT
THE-
?

KYAA!
KYAA!
KYAA!

WHO'S REALLY HERE?

SQUIRT

OH YEAH, I FORGOT... WE'RE NAKED.

PACHINK

WHAT DO YOU MEAN...

YOU WERE SELLING THOSE PHOTOS FOR 500 YEN EACH?

[ABOUT 9$]

EVEN IF THEY ARE LADIES' COATS.

WARM

WE WERE SO LUCKY TO GET THESE JACKETS.

THAT'S WHY YOU NEEDED THE MONEY?

IT WON'T BE LONG NOW. ♥

I CAN FINALLY BUY YOU THAT BOARD YOU WANTED.

YEAH, I MADE SOME MONEY, SO...

OKAY, BYE BYE.

UH-OH! THEY FOUND OUT.

YEAH, WE FOUND OUT!

NO WAY. BAD IDEA.

I WANTED TO SEE SUNAKO SO I COULD ASK HER ADVICE ABOUT MY LOVE LIFE.

NOD

NOD

REMEMBER WHEN YOU FELL IN LOVE WITH THAT GUY IN JUNIOR HIGH, SUNAKO?

PHEW

?

NO! DON'T BRING THAT UP...

HOW CAN I GET HIM TO LIKE ME MORE?

BUT... HE'LL ONLY MEET UP WITH ME IF I HAVE SOMETHING TO GIVE HIM.

WHENEVER I GIVE HIM PRESENTS, HE GETS SO HAPPY.

MASAO-KUN IS SO SWEET AND HANDSOME.

HE TOLD ME HE LOVED ME!

HE'S NOT USING ME!

I CAN'T BELIEVE HE'S USING HER LIKE THAT.

WAAHH!

H-HOW CRUEL...

HYUU

A GUY WOULD NEVER DO THAT TO THE GIRL HE LOVES.

HE'D BE TRYING AS HARD AS HE COULD TO MAKE HER HAPPY.

KYOHEI!

GLUB GLUB

KA-CHINK

WHEN YOU'RE USING A GIRL FOR MONEY, YOU GOTTA AT LEAST MAKE SURE THAT SHE FEELS LOVED.

THIS GUY SOUNDS LIKE A JERK TO ME.

WAH!

NOW WE SEE THE REAL YOU, RANMARU.

YOU'RE THE WORST, RANMARU!

HE'S NOT USING ME!

わぁん
WAH!

I KNOW HE WOULDN'T USE ME LIKE THAT!

MASAO-KUN IS A GREAT GUY!

I BET A LOT OF GROWNUPS ARE LIKE THAT.

IT'S TOTALLY WRONG!

IS THAT SO WRONG?

HYUU

...AREN'T YOU?

YOU'RE HOPING SHE ENDS UP *KILLING THAT GUY...*

I BET...

たっ...
STEP

MAYBE A LITTLE.

STOMP STOMP
どく どく

BUT I REALLY AM WORRIED ABOUT HER.

STOMP STOMP
どく どく

I'M COMING WITH YOU, YOU LITTLE FREAK.

YOU'RE THE WORST.

GO GET YOUR GUN!

THAT GIRL'S BEING ATTACKED BY A BEAR!

YUKI-CHAN...

バシャ バシャ
SPLASH SPLASH

NO! NO!

GET AWAY FROM THAT THING!

I'LL SAVE YOU!

キャ キャ
KYA! KYA!

Sunako, age 8

NO!

AHH!

IT'S THE ABOMINABLE SNOW WOMAN!

LET'S GET OUT OF HERE!

WILL YOU SHOW ME HOW TO CATCH FISH?

THIS IS WHAT YOU GET FOR JUMPING TO CONCLUSIONS.

TAKE THAT!

ヒュウウウウ
HYUU

I SAW THE WHOLE THING!

NO, THEY WERE ONLY PLAYING!

— 73 —

SNIFFLE
SNIFF

AH!
THERE
YOU
ARE.

YUKI-
CHAN!

WHOA,
WHAT'S
THAT?

HE'S
NOT
USING
ME.

FWIP

BEEP

I'LL CALL
KYOHEI.

RUMBLE
RUMBLE

RING
RING

KYOHEI
ISN'T
ANSWER-
ING.

HEY...

CLOP

CLOP

SUNAKO-
CHAN!

KYOHEI!

CLOP

SUNAKO!

AH...
CHOO.

I'M SO GLAD YOU'RE OKAY, YUKI-CHAN.

SUNAKO!

A-ARE YOU OKAY, SUNAKO-CHAN?

KYOHEI! KYOHEI!

I'M FINE.

SHUT UP.
I WAS HIT BY A FLYING TREE.

I CAN'T BELIEVE SUNAKO CARRIED YOU PIGGYBACK. YOU'RE SUCH A WUSS.

IF YOU RUB THIS ON IT, YOU'LL HEAL MUCH FASTER.

HERE.

OUCH!

OH, SORRY.

YEAH, MAYBE THAT PART WAS BRAVE, BUT...

PAT

YOU GOT HURT TRYING TO PROTECT SUNAKO?

HOW BRAVE.

GRIND GRIND

WHOA.

— 81 —

THANKS FOR HAVING US.

WELL...

I DON'T WANNA GO HOME DRESSED LIKE THIS.

BYE BYE, YUKI-CHAN.

WHAT IDIOTS.

じょぼぼ
じょ

GLUB GLUB

KACHINK

COME BACK SOON.

きゅん♥

MOVED ♥

I CAN'T BELIEVE OUR SUNAKO-CHAN IS SCARIER THAN THE REAL THING.

MAYBE WE CAN SWAP SUNAKO-CHAN WITH HER ...

MAYBE NO ONE WOULD FIND OUT.

スタスタスタスタ

SHUFFLE SHUFFLE

Chapter 25
You're More Beautiful Than a Rose

REALLY? WITH AYUYU?

YEAH, BUT I TURNED HIM DOWN.

NO WAY! WHAT A WASTE!

IS IT TRUE THAT A MOVIE DIRECTOR ASKED YOU TO BE IN HIS FILM YESTERDAY?

NOI-CHAN, NOI-CHAN!

SHE'S SO CUTE. I REALLY LIKE HER.

YEAH. BUT HE DIDN'T ASK ME TO BE IN IT. HE JUST ASKED ME TO AUDITION.

IT STARS AYUYU, AND HE WANTED ME TO PLAY HER BEST FRIEND.

A FILM?

KYAA! TAKENAGA-KUN!

GOOD MORNING, TAKENAGA-KUN.

BEHIND THE SCENES

I JUST GOT A NEW "SUPER"(?) ASSISTANT. (BUT THIS MIGHT BE THE ONLY TIME SHE HELPS ME OUT.) WHEN I WAS FINISHING UP ONE DAY, A FRIEND OF MINE (YUKO OGAWA—OFFICE WORKER) CAME TO HANG OUT AND HELPED ME WITH THE INKING. SHE'S REALLY GOOD AT INKING AND COLORING! I WAS AMAZED! ON TOP OF THAT, SHE CLEANED UP THE ROOM TILL IT SPARKLED, AND MADE COFFEE TOO. ♥

↰ SHE WAS TAUGHT BY IYU KOZAKURA (BEKKAN FRIEND).

I PROPOSED TO HER SEVERAL TIMES THAT DAY.

I WANNA MARRY A GUY!

PLEASE MARRY ME!

IN ORDER TO DRAW "AYUYU," I HAD TO STUDY UP ON "AYAYA." I REALLY FELL FOR HER. SHE'S SO CUTE. ♥♥♥

KYAA! ♥

YEAH! WE SHOULD GO!

SOUNDS LIKE A PAIN IN THE ASS TO ME.

NO WAY.

SUNAKO-CHAN'S DEFINITELY GONNA STIR UP SOME TROUBLE.

WE SHOULD GO TOO, YOU GUYS!

I'M WORRIED ABOUT SUNAKO-CHAN!

...ABOUT SUNAKO-CHAN!

THIS IS LOVE AT FIRST SIGHT, BABY.

HOW CUTE... HE'S JEALOUS.

A-AREN'T YOU THAT SUPER-FAMOUS ACTOR...?

I'M GONNA MAKE YOU THE LEAD IN MY MOVIE.

DRIP DRIP DRIP

THUMP THUMP

THUMP THUMP

SUNAKO-CHAN... SUNAKO-CHAN...

AN ABANDONED SCHOOL...

AN ABANDONED SCHOOL...

THUMP THUMP

THERE MIGHT BE CUTE GIRLS THERE. ♥

MAYBE WE CAN MEET A MOVIE STAR.

WELL, I GUESS I'M NOT DOING ANYTHING.

TA DAH.

Kyohei →

← Takenaga ← Yuki

↗ Ranmaru

Guard →

SORRY, NO UN-AUTHORIZED VISITORS ALLOWED.

THWAP

KYAA!

WELL, TOO BAD. TODAY WE HAVE TO PRETEND TO BE AYUYU OTAKUS.

I'M SCARED. I'M SCARED.

HOW-HOW CAN I LET MYSELF BE SEEN LIKE THIS?

I HATE THIS HUGE, UGLY T-SHIRT.

SNIFFLE SNIFF

SHE-SHE MUST'VE SEEN SUNAKO-CHAN.

LET'S GO.

I'M GOING HOME!

A GHOST! A GHOST!

I'M JUST AN AYUYU OTAKU, THAT'S ALL.

I CAN'T BELIEVE I DISCOVERED TWO OF THE WORLD'S GREATEST ACTRESSES...

...RIGHT HERE IN JAPAN.

MR. DIREC- TOR!

I- I CAUGHT A REALLY HOT GUY...

...IN THE BOYS' BATHROOM.

NICE WORK!

HIS HAIR AND CLOTHES ARE KINDA WEIRD, THOUGH.

KYAA! KYAA!

HE'S SO HOT! ♥

TAKE THOSE GUYS OVER TO WARDROBE.

WHAT? NO WAY!

THAT'S WEIRD.

THEY HAVE A CERTAIN GLOW ABOUT THEM.

REALLY, WE'RE JUST AYUYU FANS. WE'RE JUST OTAKUS.

SORRY. WE GOT LOST.

HEH.

HUH?

KYAA!

THEY'RE
SO HOT!

WOW,
WOW!

THEY'RE
SO COOL!

WOW!

TA-DAH

— 111 —

I WANT THIS GUY TO TAKE HIS PLACE. ♥

YOU LOOK SO BORED. ♥

HE REALLY WANTS TO WORK WITH YOU, AYUYU. ♥

DON'T RUIN THIS, NOI. REMEMBER THE YAKINIKU!

ME TOO. ♥

NO, I DON'T. LET ME GO!

THAT'S IT, NOI-CHAN.

GIVE ME THAT "FRIGHTENED SCHOOLGIRL" LOOK.

KEEP IT UP!

ALL RIGHT! WE'VE GOT OUR TITLE!

"SUNAKO-SAN—GHOST OF THE BATHROOM"!

THEY DIDN'T HAVE A TITLE YET?

THAT TITLE IS A TOTAL RIPOFF.

THIS WILL BE THE GREATEST JAPANESE FILM OF ALL TIME!

CHARISMATIC AND SEXY HIGH SCHOOL BOYS...

...A BRILLIANT AND BEAUTIFUL YOUNG ACTRESS...

...AND A REAL LIVE MONSTER.

YEAH! SUNAKO WILL SHOCK THE NATION EVEN MORE THAN "SADAKO" DID!

"SUNAKO" WILL BECOME THE VERY DEFINITION OF THE WORD "MONSTER."

NOW POKE YOUR HEAD OUT FROM THAT CORRIDOR.

OKAY, SUNAKO.

WHAT A BRILLIANT SCENE.

PRINT THAT.

MOVED ——h...

BLUSHING

Apparently she only wants to play with the real thing.

WHOOSH

AH!

CLAP

WHA-WHAT HAPPENED TO THAT ENERGY YOU HAD A MINUTE AGO?

SCIENCE LAB

CLICK

EMPTY

DISAPPOINTED

GIRLS' BATHROOM

CLICK

THEY'RE ALL OPEN.

WHOOSH

PANT

PANT

SU-
SUNAKO...

I'D GIVE UP IF I WERE YOU, MR. DIRECTOR.

I'VE NEVER SEEN HER LISTEN TO ANYBODY.

HMMPH.

WHY WON'T SHE LISTEN TO ME?

WHY ...

PLEASE COME FORTH, BEETHOVEN...

SUNAKO-CHAN SURE IS COOL.

RYUYU...

WHAT SPEED!

PANT PANT

THE SCRIPT IS READY!

BEETHOVEN...

OKAY, SUNAKO! THESE ARE YOUR LINES!

Chapter 26
Diving Panic

bed head

bed head

I KNEW IT!

WHY'D YOU EVEN ANSWER IT?

THE LAND- LADY?

THE ONLY PERSON WHO WOULD CALL THIS EARLY IS...

IT'S SO EARLY...

IT'S NOT EVEN TIME FOR SCHOOL YET.

BEHIND THE SCENES

AYUAYU WATANABE AND ATSUKO NAMBA-CHAN HELPED ME ON THIS. ♥ TWO HOT GIRLS TOGETHER AGAIN. ♥

(BUT) WHILE SHE WAS HELPING ME, NAMBA-CHAN CAUGHT A COLD, AND HER NOSE STARTED RUNNING LIKE A FAUCET. WHEN I TURNED TO LOOK BACK AT NAMBA-CHAN...

SHE'D STUFFED TISSUES UP HER NOSE.

HAHH

STOP IT, YOU HOTTIE!

NAMBA-CHAN IS A LITTLE HOTTIE BUT SHE'S ALSO VERY MASCULINE.

IT'S SO FUN DRAWING NAKED BOYS.

I DEFINITELY WANT YOU GUYS TO SEND ME PICTURES OF HOT NAKED GUYS (WITH PANTS ON).

I DON'T WANNA HAVE TO KEEP USING MY ANATOMY TEXT BOOK.

AH.

SEE? YOU'RE NOT SICK AT ALL.

ドキドキドキドキドキ
THUMP THUMP THUMP THUMP THUMP

だっ
WHOOSH

HMMPH, くぬぬ

— 133 —

MY FACE... MY FACE...

FLIP
FLOP

YOU'RE SO STUBBORN.

THE BLINDING SUN... BATHING SUITS... THE SWIM MEET...

I CAN'T GO. I WON'T GO.

I DON'T WANNA WEAR A SWIMSUIT! NOT IN FRONT OF EVERYONE!

SLIDE

TOO BAD.

TICKETS! GET YOUR TICKETS!

HOW ABOUT 80,000 YEN* FOR A THIRD-ROW SEAT?

JUST 100,000 YEN* FOR THE FRONT ROW.

WHAT? THAT'S A RIP OFF.

KYAA! I'LL TAKE ONE.

*$800

*APPROXIMATELY $1000

YOU WON'T GET ANOTHER CHANCE TO SEE ALL FOUR OF THEM TOGETHER AT ONCE!

KYOHEI TAKANO, TAKENAGA ODA, YUKINOJO TOYAMA, RANMARU MORII...

WH-WHY ARE THERE SCALPERS IN FRONT OF THE SCHOOL?

THEY'RE TALKING ABOUT US?

YEAH, SHOULD WE JUST GO HOME?

M-MAYBE WE SHOULD DITCH...

MR. PRINCIPAL!

WE-WELL... MAYBE I'LL TAKE ONE OF THOSE THIRD-ROW SEATS.

COUGH コホン

IT'S JUST A SWIM CLASS FOR GOD'S SAKE!

I'M CALLING THE POLICE!

WHAT'RE YOU SCALPERS DOING AT OUR SCHOOL?

THIS MIGHT BE YOUR ONLY CHANCE TO IMPROVE YOUR GPA.

YOU ALMOST FAILED YOUR MIDTERMS, RIGHT?

YOU GUYS ARE IN NO POSITION TO SAY THAT.

I DON'T HAVE TO WORRY, CAUSE I NEVER SKIP CLASSES.

YEAH!

WE CAN'T LET THEM FLUNK US!

LET'S MAKE SURE WE DON'T FLUNK THIS YEAR. OKAY, SUNAKO-CHAN?

HURRY UP, NOI-CHAN! COME ON!

OKAY.

WE'LL GET HER INTO THAT SWIMSUIT WHETHER SHE LIKES IT OR NOT!

WATCH HER AND MAKE SURE SHE DOESN'T RUN AWAY.

UM...

DON'T WORRY, I WON'T RUN AWAY...GO AHEAD.

WE'RE CHECKING FOR CAMERAS.

PLEASE HAVE YOUR BAGS OPEN AND READY.

CHATTER CHATTER

SORRY, WE DON'T SELL PHOTOS.

DO YOU HAVE ANY PHOTOS?

GET YOUR MERCHAN-DISE HERE!

PROGRAMS ARE JUST 300 YEN* EACH.

TAKENAGA

KYOHEI

ANMARU

*43

⌐ JUST A LIST OF NAMES.

DA-DUM

WE'RE SO LUCKY WE'RE IN THE SAME GRADE THEY ARE! ♥ WE GET TO SEE THEM UP CLOSE! ♥♥

ALL FOUR OF THEM ARE GONNA BE HERE... ALL FOUR! ♥♥

THEY CANCELLED CLASSES FOR THE WHOLE SCHOOL.

WOW... WHAT'S WITH ALL THESE PEOPLE?

PEOPLE HAVE COME FROM ALL OVER THE COUNTRY JUST TO WATCH!

IT'S NOTHING MORE THAN A SWIM CLASS, BUT...

WHAT A CROWD!

BROADCASTING CLUB

DA-DUM

DA-DUM

SQUIRT

UH... UH-HUH.

DRIP DRIP

HEY, TEACH! CAN WE JUST HURRY UP AND GET INTO THE WATER? IT'S HOT!

KYAA! KYAA!

LET'S SEE WHO CAN HOLD ONTO THIS DRY ICE THE LONGEST.

NO! I DON'T NEED ONE! I WANNA STAY AND WATCH!

GET A STRETCHER!

PARAMEDICS! WE NEED A STRETCHER!

THE TOP THREE SWIMMERS FROM EACH CLASS WILL HAVE EXTRA POINTS ADDED TO THEIR GRADES. GOOD LUCK!

WOO HOO!

...EACH PERSON MUST SWIM 25 METERS BEFORE TOUCHING THE HAND OF THE NEXT SWIMMER.

ALL CLASSES WILL COMPETE AGAINST EACH OTHER IN THIS RELAY. THE RULES ARE AS FOLLOWS...

ALL OF YOU KNOW WHEN YOUR TURN IS, RIGHT?

LET'S HAVE THE EVENS ON THIS SIDE, AND THE ODDS ON THAT SIDE.

IS EVERY-BODY READY?

OKAY.

HE'S THE VERY IMAGE OF THE RENAISSANCE MAN!

KYAA! TAKENAGA-KUN!

CALL ME A NERD AND YOU'RE DEAD, PAL.

GO FOR IT!

KYAA!

がんばって

キャ

HE'S MORE THAN JUST BRAINS.

LOOK AT TAKENAGA ODA GO! SUCH SPEED!

IT'LL CLOG THE POOL.

AH! NO CONFETTI PLEASE.

HIS NAME WAS RIGHT BEFORE MINE, AND HE SAT DOWN RIGHT IN FRONT OF ME.

JUST LIKE DURING THE FRESHMAN WELCOME CEREMONY.

I'M AFTER TAKENAGA-KUN...

I'M NEXT. ♥

AH... HE'S SO HOT. ♥

TAKENAGA-KUN. ♥

HIS HAIR WAS A LITTLE LONGER THAN IT IS NOW.

AND HE LOOKED SO HOT IN HIS SCHOOL UNIFORM.

NOI-CHAN!

— 150 —

HUH?

NOI-CHAN!

N-NOI CHAN...

NOI KASAHARA-CHAN IS NEXT, BUT SHE CAN BARELY PULL HER GAZE AWAY FROM TAKENAGA ODA.

ぱぱぱ
ちちち
SPLASH SPLASH SPLASH

COUGH COUGH

GLUB GLUB

DA-DUM

LET'S SEE HOW FAST THIS HOTTIE CAN SWIM.

SHE GETS AN A FOR STYLE!

SQUIRT

I MEAN, WHAT'S WITH THOSE GOGGLES?

SHE SAID SHE CAN'T OPEN HER EYES UNDERWATER WITHOUT THEM.

...SHE WAS A PRO OR SOME-THING.

I THOUGHT...

NEXT!

AND KYOHEI TAKANO MOVES INTO FIRST PLACE.

ど" ふ SQUIRT

TA-TAKANO... YOU'RE ONLY MAKING IT WORSE.

HEY, WAKE UP!

SQUIRT

SLAP SLAP

TAKANO! YOU'VE GOTTA SWIM AGAIN!

どくどくどく
THUMP THUMP THUMP THUMP

WHAT?

OH NO, SHE'S LOST CONSCIOUS-NESS.

SUNAKO-CHAN!

FWAP

BWAH, HA, HA!

GYAA! WHAT IS THAT?

YEAH, BUT SHE STICKS OUT LIKE A SORE THUMB.

HEH, HEH,

IT-IT ACTUALLY LOOKS GOOD ON HER... REALLY GOOD.

KYAA. ♥

SUNAKO-CHAN LOOKS SO CUTE. ♥

NAKAHARA-SAN!

...WILL BE AWARDED WITH A 50,000 YEN* GIFT CERTIFICATE TO YUGENTEI YAKINIKU RESTAURANT.

*ABOUT $500

わあああん WAH!

KYOHEI-KUN! KYOHEI-KUN!

I'LL TAKE YOU OUT TO YAKINIKU!

TAKANO IS SUCH A CHILD.

YAKINIKU!

SU-SUNAKO NAKAHARA ISN'T HERE... SHE'S NOT COMING BACK!

LET'S GO SWIMMING IN OUR POOL WHEN WE GET HOME.

THAT REALLY WAS AMAZING.

END OF WALLFLOWER BOOK 6

THANK YOU FOR READING KODANSHA COMICS.

OH, IT LOOKS
JUST LIKE ME.
♥

IF IT WEREN'T FOR ALL YOUR SUPPORT, I WOULDN'T BE
WRITING MANGA TODAY. THANK YOU SO MUCH.

OH NO...IT KIND OF SCARES ME WHEN I LOOK BACK AT
THE BONUS PAGES AT THE END OF BOOK 5 NOW.

ACTUALLY, BACK THEN I WAS EMOTIONALLY IMBALANCED.

WELL, I WAS ALREADY DEALING WITH THAT AROUND THE TIME I WAS
WORKING ON BOOK 3 OR 4, BUT ANYWAY...I WAS STILL FEELING BLUE
WHEN I WROTE THE FIRST STORY OF BOOK 6...

I REALLY DON'T WANT TO REMEMBER WHAT I WAS GOING THROUGH.

I REALLY WAS IN AN *EXTREMELY DARK* PLACE...

SIGH. I HAVE RECOVERED SINCE THEN, AND I'M FINE NOW. ♥

I STARTED TO FEEL BETTER AROUND THE TIME THAT I WAS WRITING THE
SECOND STORY IN BOOK 6.   (OCCASIONALLY I'D HAVE A RELAPSE, BUT I
                           MANAGED TO HANDLE THEM ON MY OWN.)

I'D LIKE TO THANK EVERYBODY WHO TOOK CARE OF ME.   ← VERY PERSONAL.

*THERE ARE EXTRA BONUS PAGES THIS TIME, SO
I'M GOING TO TAKE FULL ADVANTAGE OF THEM!*

THANK YOU SO MUCH FOR YOUR LETTERS. ♥

"BANSAKU-KUN: BASSIST FROM THE BAND BAROQUE.
TAKENAGA-KUN: SINGER FROM THE BAND WRISK.
YUKI-KUN: DRUMMER FROM THE BAND WRISK.

MANO-SAMA: FORMER GUITARRIST FROM THE BAND
MALICE MIZER
PRINCE MICHII: PRINCE MITSUHIRO OIKAWA

THANK YOU SO MUCH!

BANSAKU-KUN IS SO COOL! ♥

IT'S TAKENAGA-KUN! ♥

IT'S YUKI-KUN! ♥

IT'S THE GUY FROM JANNIE'S! ♥

IT'S MANO-SAMA! ♥

IT'S PRINCE MICHII! ♥

KIYOHARU! KIYOHARU! KIYOHARU! HE'S SO GORGEOUS! ♥

TO MY FANS WHO SEND ME CLIPPINGS...

YAY! ♥

I LIKE WHEN YOU GUYS SEND COLOR COPIES, TOO! THANK YOU. ♥ TO ALL THE FANS WHO SENT ME TONS AND TONS OF POSTERS OF KUROYUME... THANK YOU SO MUCH! I KEEP THEM IN SUPER GOOD CONDITION. ♥

I ENJOY RECEIVING CLIPPINGS OF MY FANS' FAVORITE BANDS TOO. ♥

ど ふ ～

SQUIRT

IT'S **A SNAPSHOT OF BANSAKU-KUN** WHEN HE WAS IN THE BAND AFTER EFFECT. ♥ (IT MUST'VE BEEN TAKEN AFTER A CONCERT.)

SUPER RARE ITEM

SPIN SPIN SPIN

WHOOAA! HE HAS RED HAIR! ♥♥♥

HE LOOKS SO YOUNG! HE'S SO CUTE! ♥♥♥

LIKE ALWAYS, PLEASE DON'T WORRY TOO MUCH ABOUT SENDING ME CLIPPINGS. I'M REALLY GRATEFUL JUST TO BE GETTING LETTERS FROM YOU. ♥

HAHH HAHH HAHH
ハハハ

SOMETIMES I REALLY FREAK OUT LIKE THAT.

DRIP
DRIP

TO ALL MY FANS WHO SENT ME MDS ♥... THANK YOU SO MUCH! I'M SO HAPPY! I FORGOT TO BUY "NIL"...THANKS TO THOSE OF YOU WHO SENT ME COMPILATION CDS.

TO THE FANS WHO GAVE ME *NIGHTMARE BEFORE CHRISTMAS* MERCHANDISE ♥...THANK YOU! I PUT ALL THAT STUFF IN MY ROOM! ♥♥♥ I LOVE JACK. ♥

THANK YOU SO MUCH EVERYBODY. ♥ YOU GUYS ARE THE SOURCE OF MY CREATIVE POWER!

I READ ALL OF YOUR LETTERS.

THERE'S JUST A LITTLE BIT OF A DELAY SINCE THE LETTERS GO THROUGH THE EDITORIAL DEPARTMENT FIRST BEFORE THEY COME TO MY HOUSE. PLEASE BE PATIENT....I WOULD LOVE TO WRITE YOU BACK ONE DAY...

I REALLY LOVE GETTING LETTERS FROM SO MANY DIFFERENT KINDS OF PEOPLE. ♥♥♥

FROM AN OFFICE WORKER, A FREELANCER, A COMMUNITY COLLEGE STUDENT, ETC.

WHOA, IT'S FROM AN ELEMENTARY SCHOOL KID. ♥

WOW, IT'S FROM A GUY! ♥

AH, IT'S FROM A HIGH SCHOOL GIRL. ♥

PEOPLE OVER TWENTY READ MANGA TOO! THERE'S NOTHING WRONG WITH IT!

OH, THERE'S A COSPLAY PHOTO! A COSPLAY PHOTO!

OH, IT'S FROM A FAN MY AGE.

I LIKE IT WHEN PEOPLE INCLUDE THEIR PHOTOS BECAUSE I GET TO SEE WHAT THEY LOOK LIKE. ♥

HMMPH, YOUNG PEOPLE THESE DAYS SEEM TO HAVE NO IDEA WHO "RANMARU" AKA "TSUCHI" IS..."RANMARU" IS THE GUY FROM THE BAND "STREET SLIDERS." HE GOES BY "TSUCHII" THESE DAYS...

GEEZ, THERE'RE STILL SO MANY PEOPLE WHO BELIEVE YUKI'S CHARACTER WAS MODELED AFTER THE BASS PLAYER FROM THAT SUPER-FAMOUS BAND. I'VE TOLD YOU GUYS SO MANY TIMES THAT HE'S NOT...

OH GOOD, THIS GIRL KNOWS WHAT I'M TALKING ABOUT. THANK GOD. IT'S NOT THAT I DON'T LIKE THAT GUY, BUT I SURE DON'T LIKE HIM ENOUGH TO USE HIM AS A MODEL OR ANYTHING. I'M KIND OF GETTING TIRED OF EXPLAINING...

SOMETIMES I MAKE COMMENTS LIKE THAT WHEN I'M READING, BUT...

SOB
ど ん

THIS IS WHAT I LOOK LIKE. ♥

(I CRY SOMETIMES, SERIOUSLY.)

THANK YOU!

MOST OF THE TIME...

ALL ABOUT "SUNAKO."

BECAUSE SHE WAS JUST AN AVERAGE "DARK LONER."

SHE WAS NORMAL IN THE BEGINNING.

*EXCERPT FROM BOOK 1. SHE MADE HER FIRST APPEARANCE.

AND THEN GRADUALLY...

...SOMEHOW...

*EXCERPT FROM BOOK 2. SHE WAS STILL TALL AROUND THIS TIME.

AND HER HEAD GOT BIGGER...

LISTEN UP, NAKA-HARA.

SHE STARTED TO SHRINK...

*EXCERPT FROM BOOK 3. SHE'S GETTING SMALLER AND SMALLER.

TA-DAH!

WHAT IS HER ACTUAL HEIGHT?

HOW DID THIS HAPPEN?

EVEN I DON'T KNOW!

ALL ABOUT "RANMARU."

WELL, I FINALLY FOUND SOMEBODY WHO WOULD MAKE A GREAT MODEL FOR RANMARU. ♥ (SINCE BOOK 4)

WHY DO I NEED A MODEL NOW...?

HE'S SUPPOSED TO BE FIFTEEN, BUT HE LOOKS WAY OLDER...

OKAY, MAYBE HE NEEDS A CHANGE.

*EXCERPT FROM THE INTRODUCTION PAGE.

I MADE HIS EYES BIGGER, ADDED SOME BANGS AND LAYERS TO HIS HAIR, AND THIS IS WHAT I CAME UP WITH...

THE GUY I CHOSE AS A MODEL HAS BIG EYES, SO...

SO I DECIDED TO GIVE HIM A NEW LOOK.

*EXCERPT FROM PAGE 27 (BOOK 5).

AHH! I'M SO SORRY!

FLAP

KYOHEI AND RANMARU LOOK EXACTLY THE SAME!

I GOT COMPLAINTS FROM FIVE OR SIX PEOPLE...

THIS IS THE LOOK I ENDED UP WITH.

HMM... HE LOOKS MUCH YOUNGER NOW. ♥

SO AFTER ALL THAT...

ANSWERS TO ALL YOUR QUESTIONS.

(1)

WHY ARE THE GUYS STILL FRESHMEN IN HIGH SCHOOL? DID THEY FAIL?

NO, THEY DIDN'T.

THEY JUST HAVEN'T AGED AT ALL.

THEY MADE IT THROUGH SUMMER AND CELEBRATED NEW YEAR'S, BUT THEY'RE STILL ONLY 15.

(2)

IS YUKI'S CHARACTER BASED ON THE BASSIST FROM THAT SUPER-FAMOUS BAND?

OKAY FINE, I'LL JUST TELL YOU WHO HE'S REALLY BASED ON.

LIKE I SAID... NO.

I'VE ALREADY DISCUSSED THIS SO MANY TIMES...

THERE'RE ACTUALLY THREE DIFFERENT MODELS FOR HIM. (KIYOHARU) AROUND THE TIME HE RELEASED "CRUEL" AND "FEMINISM," YUKI-KUN FROM THE BAND WRISK, AND REI FROM THE BAND BAROKKU.

(3)

WHO IS YOUR FAVORITE CHARACTER?

THE LITTLE VERSIONS OF SUNAKO AND YUKI...

... BECAUSE THEY'RE EASY TO DRAW.

I LOVE DRAWING THIS "YUKI" TOO.

BECAUSE I'M SUCH A BIG FAN OF THE GUY I BASED THEIR CHARACTERS ON.

I LOVE DRESSING THEM UP IN GORGEOUS COSTUMES. ♥

I ACTUALLY CAME UP WITH A LOT OF THE CLOTHES TAKENAGA AND YUKI ARE WEARING.

1. KYOHEI
2. RANMARU

BUT WHEN I'M DRESSING THEM UP IN COSTUMES, ♥ I LIKE...

*THEIR PERSONALITIES ARE SOLELY MY CREATION, AND HAVE NOTHING TO DO WITH THOSE OF THEIR MODELS.

(4)

ARE KYOHEI AND SUNAKO EVER GOING TO HOOK UP?

I HAVE NO IDEA.

(5)

PROFILE...

TAKENAGA:
BORN NOVEMBER 6, BLOOD TYPE B
NOI:
BORN SEPTEMBER 29, BLOOD TYPE A
RANMARU:
BORN OCTOBER 29, BLOOD TYPE A

I HAVE FINALLY DECIDED.
THE REST ARE STILL UNDECIDED.

DON'T ASK ME WHY THEY HAVEN'T AGED EVEN THOUGH THEY'VE ALREADY HAD THEIR BIRTHDAYS.

(6)

IS THE LANDLADY WEARING JEAN PAUL GAULTIER?

OR IS THAT SEXY DYNAMITE LONDON?

IS KYOHEI WEARING CLOTHES FROM THE BRAND ALICE AUAA?

OR IS IT H.NAOTO?

IS SUNAKO WEARING CLOTHES FROM THE BRAND NA+H? (WHEN SHE'S NOT IN SWEATS...)

THERE AREN'T ANY SPECIFIC DESIGNER BRANDS I USE WHEN I DRAW THEIR WARDROBES, BUT I DO USE MY FAVORITE DESIGNERS AS REFERENCES. SOMETIMES I LOOK AT OLD FASHION MAGAZINES FROM TEN YEARS AGO. I ALSO DESIGN THEM ON MY OWN.

I LOVE ♥ NA+H, H.NAOTO, ALICE AUAA, BLACK PEACE NOW. MY PERSONAL FAVORITE IS JEAN PAUL GAULTIER! ♥♥♥

I OFTEN GO SHOPPING AT ATELIER PIEROT INSIDE THE LAFORLE DEPARTMENT STORE IN HARAJUKU. MY FRIEND WORKS AT H.NAOTO, SO I BUY STUFF THERE TOO. IF YOU'RE EVER THERE, SAY HELLO TO MY FRIEND (A GUY). ♥

I AM A GROUPIE WHO LOVES GORGEOUS BOYS AND GIRLS!

BUT, I GUESS YOU KNOW THAT ALREADY...

I'D LIKE TO SHARE SOME STORIES FROM MY LIFE...

THEY'LL PROBABLY HELP YOU FIND OUT A LITTLE BIT MORE ABOUT ME.

WHO IS TOMOKO HAYAKAWA?

SOME THINGS NEVER CHANGE...

...PRETEND TO BE A "STALKER."

THE MOST RIDICULOUS THING I'VE DONE WHILE WAITING FOR A BAND IS...

A FEW YEARS AGO, I WAITED TO SEE KUROYUME, BUT I WAS UNSUCCESSFUL.

FOR SOME REASON, I'VE ALWAYS LOVED WAITING FOR MY FAVORITE BAND'S AFTER A SHOW.

RIGHT BEHIND YOU! ♥

HEH, HEH, HEH, HEH, HEH.
うふふふ、ふ

DO YOU KNOW WHERE I AM NOW?

HELLO, IT'S ME.

AS THE MEMBERS CAME OUT OF THE VENUE AFTER THE SHOW, I MADE A PHONE CALL.

*OF COURSE, I'M WITH A FRIEND.

YOU SHOULD TRY THIS AT YOUR OWN RISK!

(NO, I'M JUST KIDDING... ACTUALLY, YOU SHOULD NEVER DO THIS TO YOUR FAVORITE BAND.)

HERE, I BROUGHT YOU SOMETHING.

'CAUSE THAT'S NO FUN!

TAKENAGA-KUN'S REACTION WAS PRETTY LAME...

WHY CAN'T YOU JUST SHOW UP LIKE A NORMAL PERSON?

MARSHI TAKENAGA, SINGER FROM WRISK.

I HADN'T DONE THIS IN 10 YEARS... NOT SINCE THE TIME I SAW LOVE MISSILE.

KYO-CHAN WAVED AT US. ♥

GREAT SHOW!

CAR

← KAI-CHAN WHO'S IN LOVE WITH KYO.

RECENTLY, I WAITED FOR THE BAND BUG!

AN OLD STORY ②

A LONG TIME AGO...WHEN I WAS PARTYING WITH MY FRIEND'S BAND AFTER THEIR CONCERT IN SHINJUKU, THIS STUPID SINGER FROM ANOTHER BAND PICKED A FIGHT WITH US.

A GUY WHO WAS PARTYING WITH US. (THIS GUY'S UGLY TOO.) WHAT A WIMP!

SHIVER SHIVER
ぶる ぶる

UH...

MALE

WHO THE HELL DO YOU THINK YOU ARE, HUH?

HEY, YOU!

HE WAS SO UGLY. THIS IS WHAT HE LOOKED LIKE.

WHAT THE HELL DID YOU JUST SAY?

KACHING
ＳＴ４１

HE REALLY SAID THAT.

BACK OFF, BITCH!

I HAD CURLY BLONDE HAIR BACK THEN.

FINE, LET'S GO!

I REALLY SAID THAT.

YOU WANNA FIGHT? LET'S GO OUTSIDE!

HE REALLY SAID THAT.

I'VE NEVER ACTUALLY MET AN UGLY PERSON WHO WAS NICE. I'M SERIOUS!

I JUST HATE UGLY PEOPLE!

I WAS YOUNG BACK THEN... (BUT I'M STILL AFRAID I MIGHT FIGHT BACK IF SOMEBODY PICKS ON ME.)

...SOMEBODY STOPPED US, SO WE DIDN'T FIGHT AFTER ALL...

I'VE BEEN HANGING OUT IN SHINJUKU A LOT LATELY. (WELL, I JUST EAT THERE AND STUFF.)
I'VE BEEN DYING TO GET A PET...AND I'VE ALSO BEEN DYING TO MOVE.
DAMN, I WISH I COULD MOVE TO A NEW PLACE AND GET A POMERANIAN OR A POODLE!

I BECAME FRIENDS WITH MORE BANDS!

DIMARIA... THE DRUMMER IS MY FRIEND'S BUDDY. HE'S A CUTIE. THEY LOOK LIKE
YOUR TYPICAL GLAM BAND. (THEY OFTEN WEAR H.NAOTO CLOTHES ON
STAGE.) THEIR SOUND IS **POSITIVE PUNK (POSI-PUN)", AND FUN TO
LISTEN TO.

*BEFORE THE TERM "GLAM BANDS" WAS INVENTED, THIS IS WHAT WE
USED TO CALL THIS TYPE OF MUSIC. THERE USED TO BE LOTS AND LOTS
OF REALLY COOL "POSI-PUN" BANDS. THIS IS MUSIC FROM THE GOOD
OLD DAYS.

DOORMAT... THE DRUMMER IS A FRIEND OF MINE. HE'S SO CUTE ♥ AND NICE TOO!
THEY PLAY HARDCORE MUSIC. THEY'RE REALLY COOL. YOU CAN FIND
THEM IN MAGAZINES, SO CHECK THEM OUT!

CHOCOLAT S... IS A NEWLY FORMED BAND WITH THE SINGER AND GUITARIST FROM
THE BAND ASH. THE TALLER ONE, "G-KUN"... HAS BEAUTIFUL LEGS.
MY FRIEND INTRODUCED ME TO THEM OUT OF THE BLUE. THEIR SOUND
IS BASICALLY POP ROCK.

THEY'RE ALL OUT THERE PERFORMING, SO PLEASE CHECK THEM OUT!

THANK YOU SO MUCH FOR STICKING AROUND! ♥

I WONDER IF ANYONE ACTUALLY READ THE WHOLE THING...

OKAY, I'LL SEE YOU ALL AGAIN IN BOOK 7! BYE BYE. ♥

SPECIAL THANKS

MINE-SAMA,
SHIOZAWA-SAMA,
INO-SAMA,
EVERYBODY AT
THE EDITORIAL
DEPARTMENT.

MY YOUNGER BROTHER
HII (HITOSHI),
MY MOM TAKEKO,
YUKO OGAWA.

HANA-CHAN,
AYUAYU WATANABE,
ATSUKO NAMBA-CHAN,
MACHIKO SAKURAI,
IYU KOZAKURA.

CREDITS FOR THE BONUS PAGES...
TOBECHI, KAI-CHAN, OGINO-KUN, TAKENAGA-KUN, SHU-CHAN, MAKO, BUN,
EVERYBODY FROM THE HACHIOJI TEAM, AND ALL OF YOU WHO SENT ME LETTERS.

About the Creator

Tomoko Hayakawa was born on March 4.

Since her debut as a manga creator, Tomoko Hayakawa has worked on many shojo titles with the theme of romantic love—only to realize that she could write about other subjects as well. She decided to pack her newest story with the things she likes most, which led to her current, enormously popular series, *The Wallflower*.

Her favorite things are: Tim Burton's *The Nightmare Before Christmas*, Jean-Paul Gaultier, and samurai dramas on TV. Her hobbies are collecting items with skull designs and watching *bishonen* (beautiful boys). Her dream is to build a mansion like the one that the Addams family lives in. Her favorite pastime is to lie around at home with her cat, Ten (whose full name is Tennosuke).

Her zodiac sign is Pisces, and her blood group is AB.

Translation Notes

Japanese is a tricky language for most Westerners, and translation is often more art than science. For your edification and reading pleasure, here are notes on some of the places where we could have gone in a different direction in our translation of the work, or where a Japanese cultural reference is used.

Gossip Girls (page 13)
Okusama is an honorific term meaning wife, often used when referring to a married woman. Here Yuki and Ranmaru are pretending to be gossipy housewives.

Kimutaku (page 17)
Kimutaku (Takuya Kimura) is one of the most popular male celebrities in Japan. He's a member of the boy band SMAP.

Astro Boy (page 31)
Astro Boy is a famous manga/anime by Osamu Tezuka. It was published in the United States as *Astro Boy*, but the Japanese title is *Testuwan Atomu*.

Ha'penny a flower (page 52)

Sunako is actually saying "5 sen" per flower. "Sen" is a very old form of Japanese currency. One sen represents 1/100 of 1 yen. Today, the lowest denomination of currency is the 1 yen coin.

Hokkaido is alrighto (page 53)

Yuki and Kyohei are actually saying, *Hokkaido is dekkaido. Dekai zo* means "It's big." Here they have altered that phrase to create *dekkaido* so that it rhymes with hokkaido. It's a pun. We used *"hokkaido* is alrighto" to try and create a similar-sounding pun.

Abominable Snow Woman (page 57)

Sunako's friend Yuki's name is written with two characters, *yuki* and *onna,* and literally means "snow woman." Yukinojou screams out, "It's the snow woman!", but Sunako corrects him, saying that her name is actually pronounced "Yukime". The second character, *onna,* meaning woman, can also be read as "me."

*Theme from Sazae-san

Sazae-san (page 68)

Yuki-chan's cell phone rings the theme song to the long-running anime series *Sazae-san*.

Ayuyu (page 92)

Ayuyu is a play on the Japanese pop idol Ayaya.

IT STARS AYUYU, AND HE WANTED ME TO PLAY HER BEST FRIEND.

Scary School Stories (page 94)

Noi is referring to the film *Gakko No Kaidan*, *Scary School Stories*.

THE MOVIE IS JUST LIKE THAT HORROR FLICK *THE HAUNTED SCHOOL*, AND...

Otaku (page 98)

Otaku is a Japanese word for "obsessed fan." The term is generally associated with manga and anime fans, but it can be used to describe virtually any obsession. For example, an American "Trekkie" could be called an *otaku*, and a cheese lover could be called a "cheese *otaku*." In this case, the guys are pretending to be pop idol *otakus*. *Otakus* also tend to dress in very nerdy attire, hence the guys' new outfits. To learn more about the world of the Japanese *otaku*, pick up a copy of the manga *Genshiken* (published by Del Rey).

WELL, TOO BAD. TODAY WE HAVE TO PRETEND TO BE AYUYU OTAKUS.

HOW-HOW CAN I LET MYSELF BE SEEN LIKE THIS? I HATE THIS HUGE, UGLY T-SHIRT.

I'M SCARED. I'M SCARED.

SNIFFLE SNIFF

Yakiniku (page 110)

Yakiniku is Korean-style barbequed beef.
It's very popular in Japan.

Ghost stories (page 111)

This is a reference to "Toire no
Hanako-san" or "Hanako-san—Ghost of
the Bathroom," a popular urban legend
about a ghost named Hanako, who
haunts school bathrooms.

More Ghost Stories
(page 116)

Sadako is the character from the horror
movie *Ringu*, which was remade in
America as *The Ring*.

Arms Like Tyson's (page 154)

Kyohei is actually saying that Sunako's arms
are like Jyo's. Jyo is the main character in the
boxing anime series *Ashita No Jyo*.

LOOK, THAT COUPLE JUST WENT INSIDE THE HOTEL!

FRIEND

A LONG TIME AGO...I WAS WALKING DOWN THIS STREET SURROUNDED BY LOVE HOTELS IN SHIBUYA WITH THESE FIVE GUYS.

WE TOOK A SHORT CUT AFTER A CONCERT.

Love Hotels (page 172)

Love hotels are specifically designed for couples seeking privacy. They can be rented by the night or by the hour during the daytime. They often have gaudy, Las Vegas-style decor and themed rooms.

Kabuki-cho (page 174)

Kabuki-cho is the red-light district of Tokyo and is located in the Shinjuku area.

IT SEEMED LIKE GUYS FROM THE HOST CLUB'S WERE TALKING TO ME A LOT MORE THAN USUAL THAT NIGHT.

MY BACK WAS ACHING AND MY KNEES WERE SHAKING AS I WALKED BACK THROUGH KABUKI-CHO IN THE MIDDLE OF THE NIGHT.

Preview of Volume 7

We're pleased to present you a preview from Volume 7. This volume is available in English now.

TOMARE!

止まれ

[STOP!]

You're going the wrong way!

Manga is a completely different
type of reading experience.

To start at the *beginning*,
go to the *end*!

That's right! Authentic manga is read the traditional Japanese way—
from right to left. Exactly the *opposite* of how American books are
read. It's easy to follow: Just go to the other end of the book, and read
each page—and each panel—from right side to left side, starting at
the top right. Now you're experiencing manga as it was meant to be!